AYO'S AWESOME ADVENTURES IN

VANCOUVER

GATEWAY TO THE PACIFIC

www.worldbook.com

World Book, Inc.
180 North LaSalle Street
Suite 900
Chicago, Illinois 60601
USA

For information about other World Book publications, visit our website at www.worldbook.com or call 1-800-WORLDBK (967-5325).

For information about sales to schools and libraries, call 1-800-975-3250 (United States), or 1-800-837-5365 (Canada).

© 2018 (print and e-book) by World Book, Inc. All rights reserved. No part of this publication may be reproduced, stored in a retrieval system, or transmitted in any form or by any means (electronic, mechanical, photocopying, recording, or otherwise) without written permission from World Book, Inc.

WORLD BOOK and the GLOBE DEVICE are registered trademarks or trademarks of World Book, Inc.

Library of Congress Cataloging-in-Publication Data for this volume has been applied for.

Ayo's Awesome Adventures
ISBN: 978-0-7166-3636-6 (set, hc.)

Ayo's Awesome Adventures in Vancouver: Gateway to the Pacific
ISBN: 978-0-7166-3646-5 (hc.)

Also available as:
ISBN: 978-0-7166-3657-1 (e-book)

1st printing July 2018

Staff

Writer: Jamie Diehm Moore

Executive Committee

President
Jim O'Rourke

Vice President and
Editor in Chief
Paul A. Kobasa

Vice President, Finance
Donald D. Keller

Vice President, Marketing
Jean Lin

Vice President, International Sales
Maksim Rutenberg

Vice President, Technology
Jason Dole

Director, Human Resources
Bev Ecker

Editorial

Director, New Print
Tom Evans

Managing Editor, New Print
Jeff De La Rosa

Series Editor
Nathalie Strassheim

Librarian
S. Thomas Richardson

Manager, Contracts & Compliance
(Rights & Permissions)
Loranne K. Shields

Manager, Indexing Services
David Pofelski

Digital

Director, Digital Product
Development
Erika Meller

Manager, Digital Products
Jonathan Wills

Graphics and Design

Senior Art Director
Tom Evans

Senior Visual Communications
Designer
Melanie Bender

Senior Web Designer/Digital
Media Developer
Matthew Carrington

Media Researcher
Rosalia Bledsoe

Senior Cartographer
John M. Rejba

Manufacturing/
Production

Manufacturing Manager
Anne Fritzinger

Proofreaders
Mary Kieffer
Georgina Milsted

Contents

Introduction. 4

First Nations. 8

Stanley Park 10

Beaches 14

Vanier Park 16

Gardens 18

Granville Island 20

Science World 22

Chinatown 24

Gastown. 26

Vancouver Art Gallery and Robson Street. . . 28

Hockey 30

Vancouver Lookout. 32

North Shore Coast Mountains 34

Capilano Suspension Bridge. 36

Capilano Salmon Hatchery 38

Steveston Village. 40

Fort Langley National Historic Site. 42

Postcards from Vancouver 44

Glossary 46

Acknowledgments 46

Index 47

For further reading 48

Introduction

Are you ready for an adventure? My name is Ayo. I'm an aardvark, an African mammal that eats ants and termites. I'm also a tour guide traveling the world. I hope you will come with me. We are going to explore cities around the globe. In this book, we will visit the city of Vancouver, in Canada.

Canada is part of the continent of North America. Vancouver is Canada's third largest city. It is on the western edge of Canada, in the province of British Columbia. It is far from Africa, my home continent! In case you were wondering, my name, Ayo, is an African word that means *joy*.

During our travels I will introduce you to some new things and places. I'll slowly sound out words that are probably new and strange to you. When you tell your friends about your trip and use these new words, you will sound quite smart! Here's an example. The first people to live where Vancouver is now were called First Nations peoples or *aboriginal* people. That's a big word! It is said *AB uh RIHJ uh nuhl*.

We'll be talking about many things that may be new to you. If I think you may not know a word, I will explain it. If the word cannot be explained very easily, or if I use the word over and over again, I will put the word in boldface (type that **looks like this**). All boldface words will be defined in a glossary in the back of the book.

I hope someday you can travel with your family to Vancouver. You can ask to see the places we visit in this book! Then you can be the tour guide for your parents and brothers and sisters.

Vancouver information

- Population: 631,486

- Founded: 1865

- Year-round harbor: Vancouver has a natural harbor that never freezes—even though it is so far north. Ships can use the harbor the year around.

- Nickname: Ships from Vancouver trade with Japan and other nations of the Pacific Ocean rim. That is why Vancouver is called Canada's *Gateway to the Pacific.*

Canada information

- Climate: The west coast of Canada has mild summers, cool winters, and plentiful rainfall.

- Money: Canadian dollar. One hundred cents equal one dollar.

- Flag: A red maple leaf, the national symbol, in a square of white between two red stripes

flag of Canada

First Nations

I'm excited to show you around Vancouver! To start, let's find out about the people who first lived on this land thousands of years ago. Many of their descendants still live here today. In Canada, they are called First Nations people or **aboriginal** people.

We can learn more at the Museum of Anthropology. Anthropology is the scientific study of human beings and human culture. From the cliff behind the museum, you can see the Pacific Ocean below.

First Nations people fished for salmon and traveled local waters in their dugout canoes. They made these boats by hollowing out tree trunks. We can see some dugout canoes in the museum.

In the Great Hall, we can look waaay up! The poles we see are First Nations **totem poles,** each one carved from a tall tree.

Each pole is carved with different creatures, called **totems.** See if you can spot a beaver, a bear, and a frog. (No aardvarks, though.) Each animal has a special meaning and helps to tell the family story, passed down from the elders to the young ones.

Before we leave, we can explore a reconstructed village of the Haida *(HY duh)* First Nations people. Then, we're off to see more of Vancouver.

dugout canoe

Some of the totem poles here are 50 feet (15 meters) tall. That's taller than a two-story house!

Stanley Park

The people of Vancouver are nature lovers, just like me! Right next to the skyscrapers of downtown are the towering forests of Stanley Park. The park land was set aside in the late 1800's, not long after the city was founded. Stanley Park is huge, bigger than 750 American football fields!

Have you ever hugged a huge tree before? Let's take a hike on the Lake Trail or Third Beach Trail. Along these trails, we can find trees called western red cedars that reach 160 feet (50 meters) tall. These trees are three times taller than the totem poles we saw earlier.

banana slug

bald eagle

In this West Coast **rain forest,** even the ferns are taller than I am! Many animals—including slimy giant banana slugs—live among the trees and other plants in Stanley Park. It's a bit chilly for aardvarks, but bats, beavers, squirrels, and raccoons like it here.

If you see a large, messy pile of sticks in a treetop, it's probably a bald eagle nest. If you hear a sound like a squeaky wheel … look up! It's probably an eagle.

Let's rent bikes and feel the wind in our hair! We can ride around the edge of Stanley Park on the sea wall. The sea wall is an embankment built to protect the land from ocean waves. The path goes all the way around the peninsula in a big loop. It will take us about an hour. Well, maybe a little longer if we stop for ice cream.

We'll start at the park's West Georgia Street entrance. There, we're welcomed by more totem poles! Keep pedaling—during springtime you'll smell the scent of roses and rhododendrons floating on the salty ocean air.

Our path takes us beneath the Lions Gate Bridge. This **suspension bridge** carries automobile traffic across Burrard Inlet. It is named after the Lions, two mountain peaks north of Vancouver.

Keep an eye out for seals, which like to pop their heads up along the coastline or nap on a rock. We'll find beaches where we can nap or swim, too. Farther offshore, look for big ships from around the world. They are waiting their turn to load or unload cargo.

Hit your brakes for the huge Vancouver Aquarium in Stanley Park. Rescued marine mammals and other sea-living animals find a home here. We can visit beluga whales, dolphins, and sea jellies that look like they're glowing!

Beaches

On sunny summer days, it gets warm in the city. Luckily for the people who live here and visitors like us, Vancouver has nine beaches! Let's ride to some. We can follow the sea wall to English Bay.

Look at the palm trees! Even though we are far north, it hardly ever gets cold enough to snow here. Vancouver is one of Canada's warmest cities in winter.

English Bay Beach and the nearby Kitsilano Beach, at the other side of English Bay, are fun and popular places to spend the day. Should we go kayaking, play beach volleyball, or climb on the giant driftwood logs?

The logs were once tall trees in a nearby forest! After they were cut down, they traveled on a logging truck and were unloaded into the ocean. There, they were tied together and a tugboat pulled them to a mill, a factory for turning logs into lumber or paper. These driftwood logs must have broken loose. What a journey!

Palm trees can grow in Vancouver because this is a *humid oceanic climate.* That means the ocean currents help keep the air over the land a bit warmer in winter and a bit cooler in summer.

Vanier Park

Flip over a rock at Vanier Park's beach and you might be startled! Often, a little green shore crab will skitter out sideways, running for cover. The cute creatures are no bigger than a Canadian *loonie* ($1 coin) or *toonie* ($2 coin).

Let's brush the sand off our paws and walk over to see a stainless steel crab 20 feet (6 meters) tall. The enormous sculpture with raised pincers stands in front of the park's H. R. MacMillan Space Centre. It makes me think of a First Nations' legend about a crab that protected the harbor.

Inside the space center, I'll race you to the astronaut suit! Step inside and take a photo. Can you picture an aardvark as Canada's next astronaut? Of course you can! We can also touch a moon rock and try the flight simulator.

Have you heard of the famous bard, or poet, William Shakespeare? He wrote "Romeo and Juliet" and other plays that are still being performed 400 years later. Let's see one outside at a Bard on the Beach performance in Vanier Park. On Family Nights, we can get to know the play at a talk designed for kids like us. The Coast Mountains make a pretty background!

Gardens

Next, we're headed to the highest point in the city: Queen Elizabeth Park. I say we catch a taxi for the 20-minute uphill ride.

Let's check out the incredible views at the top, then go inside the unusual looking dome. It's called the Bloedel (*BLOW dehl*) Conservatory, and it is a paradise of tropical plants and flowers. It's a great place to warm up on on a wet day.

"Squawk!"
"Wheeeet!"
"Dee-dee-dee!"

Hey, it's loud in this conservatory! Hundreds of brightly colored

I want to show you a cool outdoor maze just five minutes away at the VanDusen Botanical Garden. It's an Elizabethan-style hedge maze. *Elizabethan* means from the time Queen Elizabeth I. She reigned in England, in the later 1500's. It's made of plants taller than us. Try not to get lost!

birds live here and fly around wherever they want. I see some bird friends from Africa, my home continent. Oooo, what's that? My snout is picking up some familiar flower scents.

There are three *habitats* (places where plants and animals live) beneath the dome: tropical **rain forest,** subtropical rain forest, and desert. Which one is home for a cactus? A banana plant? An aardvark? Actually, we aardvarks can live in many habitats—from dry *savannas* (grasslands) to tropical rain forests.

Granville Island

I'm getting hungry. One place **Vancouverites** go when they need fresh fruit and veggies or seafood is the Granville Island Public Market. I love to follow my nose through this place!

We can look at the shiny salmon piled up on scoops of ice, and watch the crabs poking around in big tanks. There are food booths everywhere with snacks to buy. Candied salmon, blueberries, goat cheese, brownies …

Granville Island used to be a mud flat that disappeared at high tide. In the early 1900's, the government decided to *dredge* (scoop out) False Creek and use those scoops to build up the land. Then mining and forestry companies built the warehouses and factories that are now used for shops and artist studios.

almost everything is made, grown, or caught nearby. Yummm!

Your parents will want to go shopping on Granville Island. Don't say "ugh!" yet. This place is nothing like the mall. Many of the shops here are actually studios where we can watch artists making things. There's also a Kids Market with toys and a ball pit for small folks like us. The water park here looks like fun, too.

Science World

See that giant "golf ball" at the end of False Creek? It's Science World, where we are going next. Let's hop on a miniature ferry boat cruise from Granville Island. Look at all the kayakers paddling in the shadow of downtown's skyscrapers!

Inside Science World, let's run on the giant hamster wheel and shoot water to find out about capturing energy. It's fun learning about *sustainability,* making everyday lifestyle choices that help to protect nature. Those kayakers had the right idea!

Follow me to the outdoor science park to see something strange—chickens in the middle of the city! Raising chickens for eggs is another sustainable choice, and we can learn how here. Some **Vancouverites** have backyard chicken coops.

Before we go, let's crawl through the beaver lodge. Did you know the beaver is a national symbol of Canada and appears on the five-cent coin? Beaver pelts were valuable when **aboriginal** people traded with the Europeans in the 1600's.

Locals call Science World

"the golf ball," but it's actually a *geodesic dome*, a dome built with flat triangles that fit together. Try counting them! Can you come up with the right number? (There are 766 in all!) This type of structure is super-strong because of the way the triangles naturally push against one another.

Chinatown

From Science World, we can climb aboard the SkyTrain and ride to Chinatown, only one stop away. The train runs on a track above the streets. It's fun to see the city from up here!

We'll know we're in Chinatown when we spot the Millennium Gate and the pagoda roofs, which curve up on the edges. Let's visit the markets, do a tea tasting, and eat dim sum— little buns and dumplings served in bamboo steamers. They're delivered on small carts that are pushed around the restaurant.

dim sum

Speaking of traditions, we'll find some very old gardening traditions at the Dr. Sun Yat-Sen Classical Chinese Garden. The traditions began when the Ming family ruled China, from the 1300's to the 1600's. We should pay attention to the rocks, water, and buildings, not just the plants. They all fit together. See if you can spot the influence of *yin* and *yang*, opposites that create balance. Here's one example: heavy, jagged rocks next to smooth, delicate leaves. Say "hi" to the turtles and fish in the pond!

Vancouver has one of the largest Chinatowns in North America. Why? Thousands of Chinese people emigrated to Vancouver in the late 1800's to help build railroads. Many of their **descendants** are still here.

Gastown

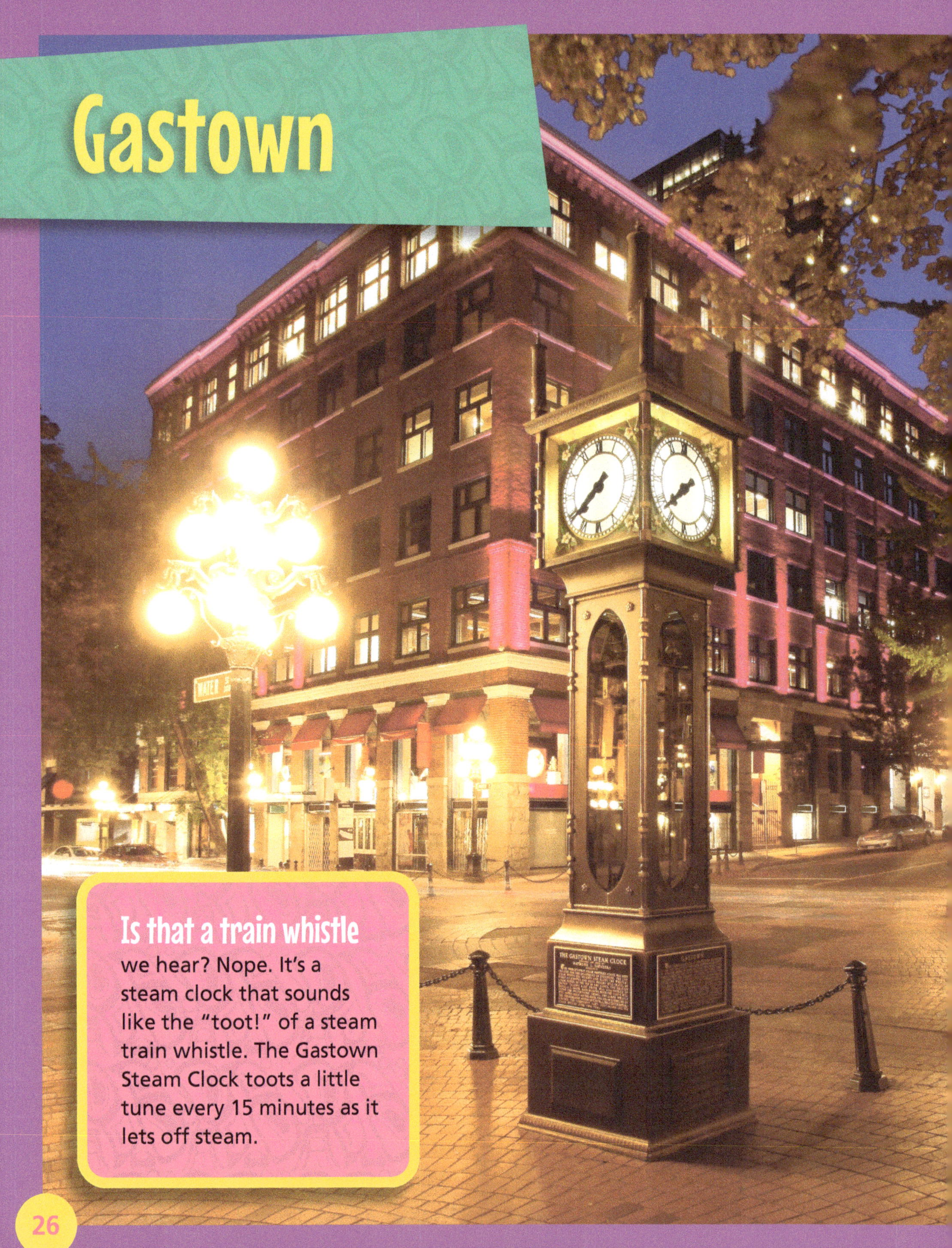

Is that a train whistle we hear? Nope. It's a steam clock that sounds like the "toot!" of a steam train whistle. The Gastown Steam Clock toots a little tune every 15 minutes as it lets off steam.

The Gastown neighborhood next to Chinatown is where the city first took root in the late 1800's. Let's go see the statue of the man who arrived here in 1867 and started building up what is now Vancouver.

His name is "Gassy" Jack Deighton. He was called "gassy" because of his long and crazy stories that must've seemed like a lot of hot air.

Jack didn't have much money, but he had whiskey, a kind of alcohol that some grown-ups drink. So he talked some sawmill workers into building his bar in exchange for whiskey. That's why he's standing on a whiskey barrel in his statue!

Jack's saloon was the first of many buildings in Gastown built with wood from nearby forests. Wood catches on fire easily, and the Great Fire of 1886 destroyed most of the city's original buildings. Many of the brick and stone buildings we see now with restaurants and shops were built just after the fire.

Vancouver Art Gallery and Robson Street

VANCOUVER ART GALLERY

Do you know anyone named Emily? I want to introduce you to a famous Canadian painter named Emily. Come with me to the Vancouver Art Gallery, where we can see the world's biggest collection of her beautiful paintings.

Emily Carr loved to draw when she was a little girl growing up on Vancouver Island in the late 1800's. She was also an adventurous traveler. She visited many First Nations villages in British Columbia.

Look at her oil paintings. You can tell she was fascinated by two things: aboriginal culture and the beautiful, green landscape of British Columbia.

ROBSON STREET

If you like fancy things, then you'll like Robson Street. It draws shoppers from around the world. Count how many languages you hear. Listen for Arabic, Mandarin, Spanish, and Japanese.

Is it lunchtime yet?

Around Robson Street, we'll find many types of international food: tacos, sushi, tapas, ramen, kimchi, and Belgian waffles. Raw oysters from Vancouver Island are a local favorite. Don't worry—there are hot dog carts here, too.

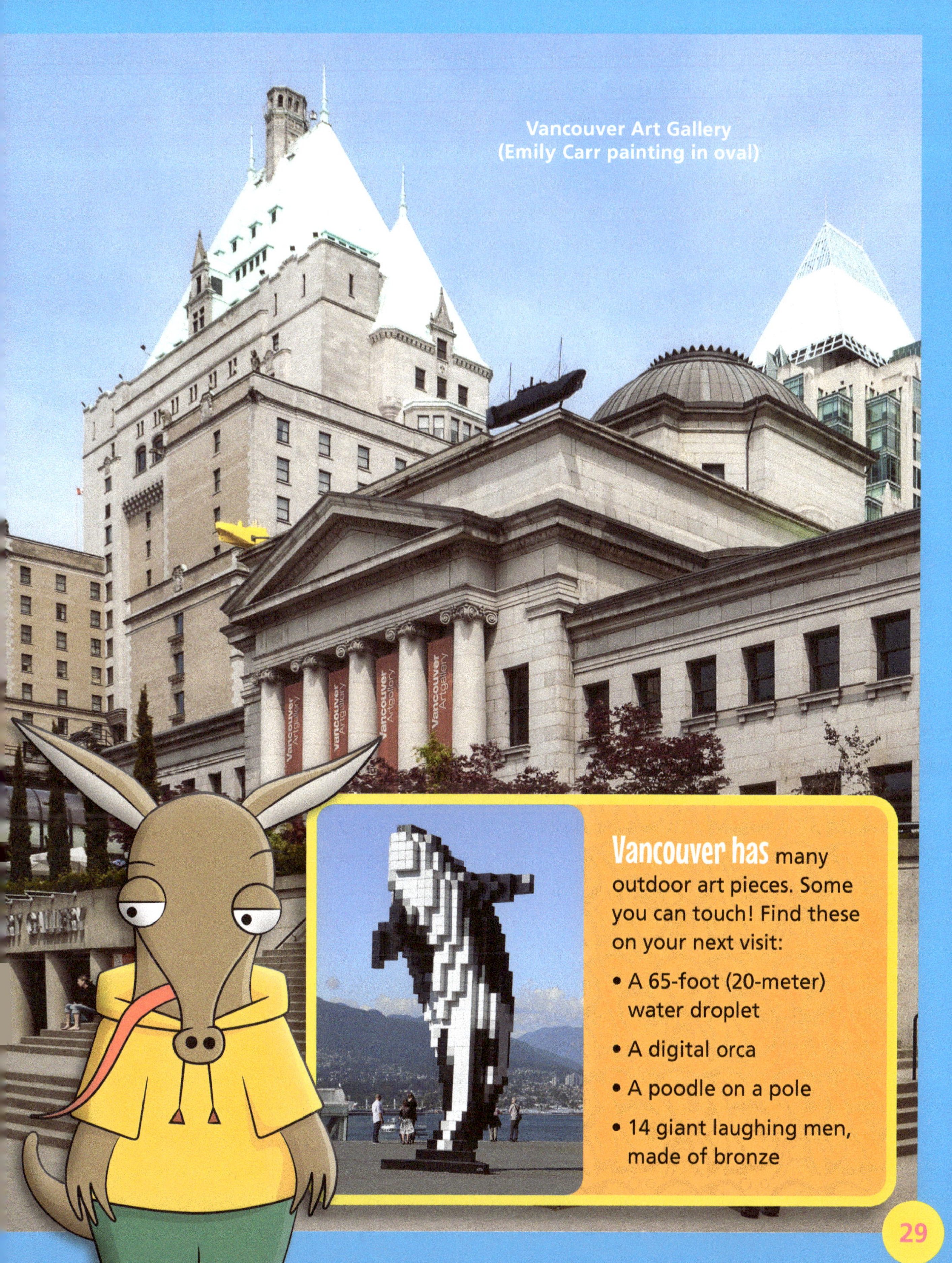

Vancouver has many outdoor art pieces. Some you can touch! Find these on your next visit:

- A 65-foot (20-meter) water droplet
- A digital orca
- A poodle on a pole
- 14 giant laughing men, made of bronze

Hockey

When many people think of hockey, they think of Canada. It's more than just a sport here. It's part of the national identity. The National Hockey League (NHL) started in Canada. And what was once printed on the $5 bill? A drawing of kids playing hockey on a pond!

Lots of Canadian kids learn to play when they are quite young on frozen ponds and backyard rinks. Some wake up when it's still dark, go to practices before school, and dream of becoming NHL players!

Vancouver cheers wildly for its hometown hockey team, the Vancouver Canucks. *Canuck* is another word for a Canadian person. That's like calling them the Vancouver Canadians! The Canucks play at Rogers Arena. If you visit during their season (from October to early April), maybe you can catch a game.

Some of Canada's proudest hockey moments happened in 2010 during the Winter Olympics in Vancouver. The men's team played the United States for the gold medal and won in overtime. The Canadian women's team beat the U.S. team to win the gold medal, too!

At the BC Sports Hall of Fame, we can pretend to be Olympians. ("BC" stands for British Columbia.) Let's see the Olympic torch and gold medals, then stand on the actual medal winners' podium!

VANCOUVER CANUCKS
PRESIDENTS' TROPHY
CANUCKS
PRESIDENTS' TROPHY
PAVEL BURE
MARKUS NASLUND
TREVOR LINDEN
12 STAN SMYL
ROGERS ARENA
POWERPLAY

Vancouver Lookout

We've seen Vancouver from the ground looking up. Now let's go see it from the sky looking down. Follow me to the Vancouver Lookout. In a high-speed glass elevator, we'll zoom to the observation deck 553 feet (169 meters) in the sky.

Imagine more than 30 of my African giraffe friends standing on top of another. That's how high we are.

This deck is a cool place to see the mountains, the ocean, and the clouds. If we're here at the right time, we can watch float planes landing or taking off for distant islands and remote fishing lodges. Cruise ships headed to Alaska depart from that terminal with the big white sails.

We can see Vancouver's **sustainable** planning from up here! The tall glass buildings have enough space between them so the people who live and work downtown can still see nature. Trees are planted along the streets and on rooftops. One rooftop is even covered in grass! It works like a jacket, helping to keep the convention center warmer in winter and cooler in the hot summer sun.

Did you know there's an amusement park downtown? We can get another bird's-eye view of the city from atop a giant roller coaster or high-flying swings at Playland.

North Shore Coast Mountains

Let's explore those Coast Mountains we keep seeing! They're less than 30 minutes away, on Vancouver's North Shore. We can drive across the Lions Gate Bridge from Stanley Park or catch a passenger ferry called the SeaBus.

GROUSE MOUNTAIN

Climb aboard the *gondola* (a car that hangs from a cable) that takes people up Grouse Mountain. On the way up, look for Vancouver Island and the Cascade and Olympic mountains. Grouse Mountain is known for skiing, hiking, and *zip lines*, long cables you can strap onto and whoosh down the mountainside. My favorite, though, is seeing rescued bears at the grizzly refuge. There aren't any wild

grizzlies on the North Shore, but black bears live here.

CYPRESS MOUNTAIN

Olympic athletes competed on Cypress Mountain in 2010. We could ski or snowboard like them, but let's zoom down the slopes on an inner tube instead. A lift will pull us back up to the top after each run.

MT. SEYMOUR

Want to tramp through an ancient forest of western hemlock, cedar, and Douglas fir wearing a pair of snowshoes? Imagine a pair of tennis rackets strapped to your boots! Snowshoes spread out our weight so we don't sink into the snow. Native Americans used to make them with animal skins stretched across a frame.

Capilano Suspension Bridge

Where do you think water goes when the snow melts on the Coast Mountains or when it rains? The water rushes downhill in streams and rivers. The rivers then empty into the ocean. One of those rivers is the Capilano. A fun way to see the river is swaying above it on the Capilano Suspension Bridge.

Are you the kind of kid who steps carefully onto a wobbly bridge or the type who tries to get it swinging? Heights aren't my thing. The word *aardvark* means *earth pig,* and I'd rather be on the ground. This bridge sways so high in the air! The Statue of Liberty would fit below.

After we cross the bridge, let's follow the Cliffwalk path. This pathway grips the steep canyon wall. Treetops Adventure is up next—seven smaller bridges rising into the evergreens. My heart is racing! Back on the ground, we can hike **rain forest** trails and explore the First Nations center.

The Capilano Suspension Bridge hangs without any towers to support it. Each end is anchored into concrete—the only thing that holds it up. The Lions Gate **suspension bridge** is a little different. Its cables transfer the weight to towers that support most of the load.

Capilano Salmon Hatchery

If we take a 10-minute hike upstream from the **suspension bridge,** we'll find the Capilano Salmon Hatchery. The Capilano River is one of many rivers around Vancouver where big salmon swim and leap upstream. They are working hard to get to the place where they *spawn* (lay eggs).

At the hatchery, we can watch salmon underwater through windows. Salmon climb fish "ladders" by jumping from one pool to the next higher pool.

Look at all the big tanks outside with thousands of salmon in them! Every spring, the hatchery releases salmon ready to make their journey to the ocean.

A salmon's life

1. After they hatch, salmon spend a year or more in the river before swimming out to sea.

2. Some kinds of salmon live in the ocean for 1 1/2 years, but others live there for 8 years.

3. Somehow, their bodies know when it's time to return to the same exact river where they hatched.

4. They fight their way upstream, or "run," in summer and fall.

5. By this time, the males' bodies have really changed, with bright colors and hooked jaws.

6. The females spawn in the gravel riverbed, the males fertilize the eggs, then all the grown-ups die.

Steveston Village

We were just on the north side of Vancouver. Now let's explore the south side in a historic village called Steveston.

Follow the smell of saltwater—and the seagull noise—to the Steveston docks. We'll walk past commercial fishing boats and can peek inside to see the salmon, *prawns* (large shrimp), halibut, and cod caught today!

In the late 1800's, Steveston was the West Coast's largest fishing port. More than 15 canneries lined the waterfront. A cannery is a place where fish and other seafood are cut into pieces and packed into containers … a very slimy business!

One of those canneries, the Gulf of Georgia Cannery, is now a museum. Let's go in! Look at the long lines of cans. Can you imagine working there, surrounded by steam, clattering machines, and stinky fish? No, thank you. Besides, I think my claws might be a problem. You can try out a cannery worker's tool known as a *peugh (pew),* a sharp spear used to move slippery fish.

The Fraser River flows into the ocean at Steveston. If you guessed that salmon swim upstream to spawn here, you're right! That makes Steveston a good place to go fishing—and a great place to eat *fish and chips*, deep-fried fish and French fries.

Fort Langley National Historic Site

Let's end our visit with a trip up the Fraser River. About 30 miles (50 kilometers) east of Vancouver, we'll find the Fort Langley National Historic Site. It is surrounded by a tall wooden *palisade* (fence of sharpened wood posts), but I think they'll let us in.

Fort Langley was a trading fort built by the Hudson's Bay Company in 1827. Back then, the French-Canadians of the company traded with First Nations people in the area. The traders gave the First Nations people wool blankets, a red coloring called *vermillion,* and tobacco in exchange for beaver pelts, salmon, and cranberries.

The people who work here are dressed like they're from the 1800's. Do you hear that clanging? It's coming from the blacksmith's shop. Watch the flying sparks as the metal is hammered and shaped into tools. It's like we time-traveled back to the year 1827!

The Hudson's Bay Company traders sent beaver *pelts* (skin with the fur left on) to England, where they were turned into felt hats. The **aboriginal** people received wool blankets, which they made into coats. We could buy a similar blanket today at "Hudson's Bay" department store—the same Hudson's Bay Company that set up trading posts nearly 200 years ago!

First Nations crafts
Vancouver Lookout
Beaches
Capilano Suspension Bridge

Gardens
Thanks for
exploring Vancouver
with me. I hope to
see you soon!
Ayo

Glossary

aboriginal *(AB uh RIHJ uh nuhl)* Of the first human beings to live in Canada. Aboriginal people are also called First Nations.

descendant *(dih SEHN duhnt)* An offspring; child, grandchild, great-grandchild, and so on

rain forest *(rayn FAWR ihst)* A woodland of tall trees growing in an area of plentiful rainfall

suspension bridge *(suh SPEHN shuhn brihj)* A type of bridge that has its road or pathway hung on cables and chains, often between towers

sustainable *(suh STAY nuh buhl)* Following principles of conservation and ecological balance to help protect the environment

totem *(TOH tuhm)* A symbol for a tribe, clan (group), or family

totem pole *(TOH tuhm pohl)* A series of totems carved into an upright pole

Vancouverite *(van KOO ver yt)* A person who lives in Vancouver

Acknowledgments

Cover © Romakoma/Shutterstock
Ayo artwork by Matthew Carrington

4-7   © Shutterstock
8-9   Leoboudv (licensed under CC BY-SA 3.0)
10-11   © Shutterstock; © Dee Golden, Shutterstock; © Daniel Sobolic, Shutterstock
12-13   © Steve Smith, Dreamstime; © Regien Paassen, Shutterstock; © Shutterstock
14-15   © Leo Bruce Hempell, Dreamstime; © Karamysh/Shutterstock
16-17   © Lissandra Melo, Shutterstock; © Pete Spiro, Shutterstock
18-19   © Ronnie Chua, Shutterstock; © Fred Goldstein, Shutterstock; © All Canada Photos/Alamy Images
20-27   © Shutterstock
28-29   © Shutterstock; © ART Collection/Alamy Images; © Meunierd/Shutterstock
30-31   © Meunierd/Shutterstock
32-33   © Vkyryl/iStockphoto; © Fgcanada/Dreamstime
34-37   © Shutterstock
38-39   Ruth Hartnup (licensed under CC BY 2.0)
40-41   © Ronnie Chua, iStockphoto; © Volodymyr Kyrylyuk, Shutterstock
42-43   © Ian Mcdonald, Dreamstime; © Rieke Photos/Shutterstock

Index

A

aboriginal people. *See* First Nations people

B

banana slugs, 11
beaches, 12, 14-15, 44-45
bears, 34-35
beavers, 22
blacksmith's shop, 42-43
Bloedel Conservatory, 18-19
British Columbia, 6, 28

C

Canada, 6-7
canoes, dugout, 8, 9
Capilano River, 38-39
Capilano Salmon Hatchery, 38-39
Capilano Suspension Bridge, 36-37, 44
Carr, Emily, 28, 29
cedar trees, 10
chickens, 22
Chinatown, 24-25
Cliffwalk path, 36
Coast Mountains, 17, 34-36
crabs, 16, 20
Cypress Mountain, 35

D

Deighton, "Gassy" Jack, 27
dim sum, 24
Dr. Sun Yat-Sen Classical Chinese Garden, 24

E

eagles, bald, 11
Elizabeth I, Queen, 18
English Bay Beach, 14

F

First Nations people, 6, 10, 16, 28, 35, 36; and trade, 22, 42; crafts, 8-9, 44
fishing, 8, 40-41
food, 20-21, 24, 28, 40-41
Fort Langley National Historic Site, 42-43
Fraser River, 41, 42

G

gardens, 18-19, 24, 45
Gastown, 26-27; Steam Clock, 26
geodesic dome, 23
Granville Island, 20-21
Great Fire of 1886, 27
Grouse Mountain, 34-35
Gulf of Georgia Cannery, 40

H

H. R. MacMillan Space Centre, 16-17
Haida people, 8
hockey, 30-31
Hudson's Bay Company, 42

K

Kitsilano Beach, 14

L

Lions Gate Bridge, 12-13, 34, 37
logging, 14
loonie (coin), 16

M

Mount Seymour, 35
Museum of Anthropology, 8-9

N

National Hockey League (NHL), 30

O

Olympic Games (Winter, 2010), 30, 35

P

pagodas, 24-25
palm trees, 14-15

Q

Queen Elizabeth Park, 18-19

R

rain forests, 11, 19, 36
Robson Street, 28
Rogers Arena, 30-31

S

salmon, 8, 20, 38-41
Science World, 22-23
Shakespeare, William, 17
SkyTrain, 24
Stanley Park, 10-13, 34
Steveston Village, 40-41
suspension bridges, 12-13, 36-37, 44
sustainability, 22, 32

T

totem poles, 8-9, 12

V

Vancouver, 4-7
Vancouver Aquarium, 13
Vancouver Art Gallery, 28-29
Vancouver Canucks, 30-31
Vancouver Lookout, 32, 44-45
VanDusen Botanical Garden, 18
Vanier Park, 16-17

Y

yin and yang, 24

For further reading

Books

Manzione, Lisa. *The Adventures of Bella & Harry: Let's Visit Vancouver!* Delray Beach, Florida: Bella & Harry, 2014.

Marcelino, Pedro F. *Junior Jetsetters Guide to Vancouver.* Toronto: Junior Jetsetters Publishing, 2010.

Robbins, Jody. *25 Places in Canada Every Family Should Visit.* Victoria, British Columbia: TouchWood Editions, 2017.

Websites

Aboriginal people
https://www.aadnc-aandc.gc.ca/eng/1315444613519/1315444663239

Hockey
https://www.hockeycanada.ca/multimedia/kids/

Salmon life cycle
http://www.pac.dfo-mpo.gc.ca/fm-gp/species-especes/salmon-saumon/facts-infos/cycle-eng.html

www.ingramcontent.com/pod-product-compliance
Lightning Source LLC
Chambersburg PA
CBHW050554290625
28882CB00023B/1362